Estate Planning For Married Couples

How to Get Your Affairs in Order
And Achieve Peace of Mind

JULIE A. CALLIGARO

ISBN: 1-890117307
ISBN-13: 978-1890117306

WHY READ THIS BOOK

Most of us avoid *estate planning*, which is another name for getting our affairs in order, until we face a life-changing event such as:

The birth or adoption of a child; the diagnosis of an illness that threatens disability or death; a family member or close friend dies unexpectedly; a new marriage with one or both spouses having children from a previous marriage. And sometimes it's just because we're about to take a trip.

I congratulate you because you've decided to take action rather than wait for a crisis or emergency. This book will help you get your affairs in order, make things as easy as possible for you your family at your incapacity and/or death and bring you peace of mind.

This book does NOT include fill-in-the-blank Wills, Trusts, Powers of Attorney or Guardianship forms. If you want a do-it-yourself estate plan this is not the book for you. In my 30 years as an estate planning and probate attorney, I've seen only regret and heartache from do-it-yourself legal forms.

I have, however, developed forms and checklists that will save you time and energy as you work through the estate planning process. The forms and checklists are free at www.wsbforms.com/married. Download the forms and checklists and use them as you work through the action steps in each Chapter.

TABLE OF CONTENTS

THE ESTATE PLANNING STEPS

Step 1. Have Your Financial Information at Your Fingertips.

Step 2. Learn About the Estate Planning Tools:

- Wills
- Trusts
- Powers of Attorney
- Living Will
- Beneficiary Designation
- Joint Ownership

Step 3. Consider the Issues Unique to Your Situation. Do you have?

- Minor Children
- Adult Children
- No Children
- A Blended Family

Step 4. Choose an Estate Planning or Elder Law Attorney and Schedule an Appointment.

Step 5. Follow Through.

List of Forms and Checklists:

To download the forms and checklists click on: <u>www.wsbforms.com/married</u>

Forms Related to Finances

Excel Spreadsheet of Assets and Debts

Insurance Policies Inventory

Pension Plans Inventory

Forms Related to Minor Children

Parental Consent Form Minor Children

Medical Information Minor Children

At Disability and Death

Who to Contact in an Emergency

Location of Your Documents

Family Advisors

Funeral and Burial Information

Take to the Meeting with an Estate Planning Attorney

Questions to Ask the Attorney

Estate Planning Questionnaire

Excel Spreadsheet of Assets and Debts

Insurance Policies Inventory

Pension Plans Inventory

Checklist of Documents

Optional but Useful

Excel Spreadsheet of Income and Expenses

ONE

HOW TO HAVE YOUR FINANCIAL INFORMATION AT YOUR FINGERTIPS

This book is a practical guide to estate planning. But to formulate a complete and accurate estate plan, you need to begin with your financial information. Here's why.

It's impossible for you and your attorney to create an intelligent estate plan that transfers your assets at your death if you don't know precisely what assets you have. It's impossible for you and your attorney to be certain that your beneficiary designations are up-to-date if you don't know who the current beneficiaries are. And it's impossible to determine if your assets are titled correctly if you're not sure whose name or names are on the titles.

That's why to establish an accurate and complete estate plan, you need a list or inventory of your assets and debts which includes the name or names currently on the title of each asset. And you need a list or inventory of your life insurance policies and your retirement plans including the names of the primary and secondary beneficiaries.

Fortunately there are forms that will help you prepare these lists. Go to www.wsbforms.com/married.

Download and complete the forms listed below this paragraph. They are self-explanatory and worth the time it will take you to fill in the requested information.

- Excel Spreadsheet of Assets and Debts
- Insurance Policies Inventory
- Pension Plans Inventory

If you ignore everything else except this one Chapter, the book will have paid for itself.

TWO

WHO WILL MANAGE YOUR FINANCES AND MAKE MEDICAL DECISIONS FOR YOU?

You will discuss this issue in detail with your attorney. My goal is to help prepare you for that discussion.

Who will manage your finances if you become incapacitated?

You can appoint a spouse, child, family member of friend to manage your finances if you become incapacitated with a financial power of attorney or a living trust.

Financial Power of Attorney

A financial power of attorney is a legal document that appoints someone you TRUST as your "agent" should you become incapacitated. You may need this person to pay your bills, do your banking, file your tax returns, collect rents, etc. A power of attorney takes effect either at the time you sign the document or at the time you become incompetent. Be sure to discuss these options with your attorney.

Four Important Points About Financial Powers of Attorney:

1. You cannot sign a Power of Attorney if you are incompetent, so advance planning is essential.

2. A Power of Attorney gives your agent the power and authority over your finances, so you must choose a person you **trust.**

3. Name an alternate in case the first person you name is not available or able to act as your agent.

4. A Power of Attorney terminates at your death.

Living Trust (which is discussed in detail in the next Chapter)

A living trust is an alternative to a financial power of attorney because if you become disabled or incompetent, your successor trustee is authorized to take over the management of the trust assets during your disability or incompetence.

Who Will Make Medical Decisions for You if You Cannot Make Them for Yourself?

Medical Power of Attorney

A medical power of attorney is a legal document that appoints someone you TRUST to make medical decisions for you if you cannot make the decisions for yourself. You can appoint your spouse, child, family member or friend. A medical power of attorney is also known as health care proxy and patient advocate designation.

Four Important Points About Medical Powers of Attorney:

1. You cannot sign a Power of Attorney if you are incompetent, so advance planning is essential.

2. A Power of Attorney gives your agent the power and authority to make your medical decisions, so you must choose a person you **trust.**

3. Name an alternate in case the first person you name is not available or able to act as your agent.

4. A Power of Attorney terminates at your death.

Living Will

A living will is a document that expresses your wishes concerning the use of artificial or life-support measures if there is no reasonable expectation you will recover.

I strongly recommend that you have a face to face discussion about end of life decisions with the people you appoint as your medical power of attorney. If your spouse or children have to make a "turn off the machine" decision, it will be easier for them if you've told them how you feel and what you want and expect them to do.

Estate Plan

Financial and Medical Powers of Attorney are two of the documents included in an "Estate Plan." The other Estate Plan documents are discussed in the next Chapters.

Action Plan

- Your attorney will prepare the necessary documents that will appoint someone you trust either by a Power of Attorney or by a Living Trust to manage your finances if you become incapacitated or incompetent.
- Your attorney will prepare the necessary documents that will appoint someone you trust to make medical decisions for you if you cannot make the decisions for yourself.
- Have a face to face conversation with the people you've named as your medical power of attorney.

THREE

HOW TO TRANSFER ASSETS AT YOUR DEATH

YOU HAVE OPTIONS

You will discuss this issue in detail with your attorney. My goal is to help prepare you for that discussion.

There are five ways to transfer assets at death:
1. Beneficiary Designation;

2. Joint Ownership;

3. Will;

4. No Will;

5. Living Trust.

Some combination of these documents, together with Financial and Medical Powers of Attorney, constitute an "Estate Plan."

1. Beneficiary Designation

Certain types of assets allow you to name a beneficiary who will receive the asset at your death. Assets that pass by beneficiary designation go directly to the beneficiary thereby avoiding Probate.

However, if your beneficiary dies before you and you have not named a secondary (also called contingent) beneficiary the asset must go through Probate.

Examples of assets that allow you to name a beneficiary are: life insurance policies, annuities, IRAs, and certain types of bank and brokerage accounts. Bank and brokerage accounts that allow you to name a beneficiary or beneficiaries are called "Transfer on Death" (TOD) or "Pay on Death" (POD).

2. Joint Ownership

If an asset is titled in your name and the name of another person as "joint tenants with rights of survivorship," the asset passes directly to your joint tenant(s) at your death thereby avoiding Probate. Examples are deeds, bank and brokerage accounts, savings bonds and stock certificates.

If, however, your joint tenant dies before you die, the asset will then be in your name alone. Unless you add a new joint tenant, the asset must go through Probate at your death.

There are risks and disadvantages holding an asset as a joint tenant with someone other than your spouse. They are:

1. To sell the asset you must have your joint tenant's cooperation and participation. For example, if you are selling your house and your son is a joint tenant, he and his wife must also "sign off" before you will be able to complete the sale.

2. The asset is vulnerable to your joint tenant's divorce, lawsuits and creditors. For example, if your daughter is a joint tenant on your bank account and she is sued, her creditors can collect from your bank account.

3. Will

If your assets pass to your spouse, children, family member or friend by Will, THE ASSETS MUST GO THROUGH PROBATE. The preceding sentence may surprise you as most people believe that if they have a Will, they have avoided Probate. Not true. If assets pass by Will, they must go through Probate.

Why so? If, at your death, there are assets in your name alone, only a Probate Court can legally transfer those assets to the persons named in your Will.

The purpose of a Will is to tell the Probate Court who is to receive your assets at your death, who is to administer your estate (the personal representative or executor) and who is to be guardians of minor children.

4. No Will

If, at your death, there are assets in your name alone and you do not have a Will, your assets must pass through Probate and the laws of the state in which you live will dictate who will receive them.

5. Living Trust

A Living Trust is similar to a Will because it names who is to receive your assets at the death of you and your spouse and who is to administer the Trust (the trustee).

You create a Living Trust by signing a legal document called a Trust Agreement. You and your spouse are the trust makers, the trustees and the beneficiaries. If you and your spouse each have your own trust, you and your spouse will be the trustees of both trusts and the beneficiaries of both trusts. You can change or revoke your trust at any time.

As the trustee and beneficiary you manage and have full use of the trust assets during your lifetime. If you become incompetent and at your death, the person you have named as your successor trustee takes over.

A living trust is especially useful if your become disabled or incapacitated because your successor trustee is authorized to take over the management of the trust assets. If a successor trustee does take over because of your illness or incapacity, the trust assets are used *exclusively* for your support and care and that of your spouse.

A Trust CAN Avoid Probate

When you and your spouse are both deceased, your successor trustee distributes the assets to the person or persons you've named as the beneficiaries of your trust. If your assets are in the name of your Trust, the assets will pass directly to the trust beneficiaries avoiding Probate. However, if your assets are not in the name of your Trust, the assets must first go through Probate to get to your trust beneficiaries.

Your attorney will transfer your assets to your trust by changing the title of the asset from your name (and your spouse's name if he or she is also on the title) into the name of your trust. If you have a trust but your assets have not been transferred into the trust, contact your attorney immediately.

The primary difference between a will and a trust is a trust can avoid probate. A will cannot avoid probate.

Other Reasons to Use a Living Trust

Trusts are used for reasons other than avoiding probate, for example: for a married couple, trusts can reduce or eliminate estate or death taxes (See Chapter Four). If you're in a marriage that blends children from prior relationships, a trust or trusts can provide for the children of both spouses regardless of the sequence of deaths. Trusts are also used to safeguard distributions to minor children and to safeguard governmental benefits that are or may be received by disabled children and/or adults.

Avoiding Probate

You will avoid Probate if:

1. Your assets pass by beneficiary designation and the beneficiary

survives you.

2. You hold title as joint tenant with right of survivorship and the joint tenant is alive.

3. You have a living trust and your assets are in the name of your trust.

Action Steps

- Your objective is to set up an estate plan that transfers your assets at your death.
- Your action plan is to consider the options presented in this Chapter so you are prepared to meet with an estate planning attorney.
- Your attorney will prepare the necessary documents that will transfer your assets at your death.
- How to find an attorney, what questions to ask and what information to take to the first meeting is discussed in Chapter Five.

FOUR

TAXES AND "DEATH TAXES"

You will discuss this issue in detail with your attorney. My goal is to help prepare you for that discussion.

Locate Tax Returns from Prior Years

If, because of disability, you are unable to file your tax returns, your spouse or children will have to file them for you. Your tax returns from prior years will help them.

Locate your tax returns from the past three years. Insert each year's returns in a separate folder and label the folders. File the folders with your other important documents.

Implement a System to Collect Information for Future Returns

Whether you or someone else will be filing next year's tax returns, streamline the process by having information about the year's income and deductions accessible and organized. As you receive 1099s from your employer(s) and financial institutions, insert them in a labeled folder. Also collect information about the assets you sold during the year. At year-end you should have all the information you will need to file your tax returns in the folder. As soon as you have all of the necessary information, schedule a meeting with your tax advisor (or prepare and file the returns yourself.)

Gift and Estate Taxes (Death Taxes)

As I write this in 2012, each one of us can transfer $5,120,000 at death without paying estate taxes (often called "death taxes"). A married couple, implementing an estate plan in which **both** the husband and the wife have a revocable living trust, with the appropriate provisions, can double the amount they can transfer to their beneficiaries without paying estate taxes.

HOWEVER, the estate tax laws change as of January 1, 2013 and the estate tax exemption will drop from $5,120,000 to $1,000,000. In other words, after January 1, 2013, a husband and wife with the proper trusts can transfer $2,000,000 to their beneficiaries estate tax free. Keep abreast of changes in the estate tax laws because changes in these laws may necessitate changes in your estate plan.

Action Plan

- Set up a system to collect this year's tax information.
- Collect your tax returns from previous years and file them with your important documents.
- Referring to your Inventory of Assets and Debts, what is the total value of your assets? Does that dollar amount puts you in the "estate tax bracket?"
- If you are in the estate tax bracket, your attorney will prepare the necessary documents that will maximize the amount you and your spouse can pass at your death estate tax free.

FIVE

WHO SHOULD PREPARE YOUR ESTATE PLAN?

Who Should Prepare Your Estate Plan?

I recommend that you hire an *experienced* estate planning or elder law attorney to prepare the legal documents that will make up your estate plan. It's penny-wise and pound-foolish to "do-it-yourself."

However, I also recommend that YOU control your estate plan. You tell your attorney what you want your plan to accomplish. Ask your attorney what options you have, including the cost, and the positives and negatives of each option. Then you decide (not your attorney) which options best meet your objectives.

How to Locate an Attorney

You want an estate planning or elder law attorney - an attorney who does estate planning for a living and not as a sideline. Your best source of information is a satisfied customer, so ask family and friends for suggestions. Your accountant and financial planner are also good sources of recommendations.

Another source is your local Bar Association; call and ask for the names of estate planning and elder law attorneys in your area.

Cost of the Initial Consultation

Most estate planning and elder law attorneys do not charge for an initial consultation. Take advantage of a no cost consultation. It will give you the opportunity to judge whether you feel comfortable with the attorney and what his or her fees will be for the documents that you need prepared.

I'm sorry to say that some attorneys do not treat their clients well. If you are not treated respectfully by the attorney and staff; if you are kept waiting for an unreasonable amount of time; if fees are not readily and thoroughly explained; if your estate plan cannot be done in a timely manner and if your phone calls are not returned promptly, find another attorney. There are lots of us out there.

Questions to Ask the Attorney

1. Is estate planning your primary area of practice?

2. How do you charge, flat fee or hourly?

3. If the charge is hourly, what is your best estimate of the total fee?

4. If I have questions will I be able to contact you personally by phone or email?

5. Do you return calls or emails promptly?

6. If you will be drafting a revocable living trust, will you also prepare the documents that will transfer our assets to the trust? Is that included in the fee for the trust or is there an additional cost? **If the attorney will not prepare the documents that transfer your assets to your trust, find another attorney!**

7. How long will the process take from start to finish? If you are about to take a trip and want your estate plan in place before you leave, be sure you tell the attorney at your first meeting.

Before You Meet with an Attorney

Go to www.wsbforms.com/married and download and fill in the forms in the "Take to the Meeting with an Estate Planning Attorney" section. Fill in the blanks and take them to your first meeting with an estate planning attorney.

Action Steps

- Ask family, friends or co-workers for the name of an estate planning or elder law attorney.

- Schedule an appointment with the attorney and confirm that the initial consultation is free.

- Before you meet with the attorney go to www.wsbforms.com/married and download the forms in the "Take to the Meeting with an Estate Planning Attorney" section. Fill in the blanks and take the forms to the meeting with the attorney.

- Meet with the attorney and discuss your objectives and your options.

- If you like the attorney, feel satisfied that you understand your options and the fee is fair, engage the attorney to prepare the documents needed to create your estate plan.

- Put the documents in a safe place. Tell your children where to find the documents and make certain they can access them.

ONLY ONE OF THE NEXT FOUR CHAPTERS APPLIES TO YOU. GO DIRECTLY TO THE CHAPTER THAT DISCUSSES YOUR SITUATION.

SIX

ESTATE PLANNING FOR A MARRIED COUPLE WITH MINOR CHILDREN

You will discuss your family structure in detail with your attorney. My goal is to help prepare you for that discussion.

What is an Estate Plan for a Married Couple with Minor Children?

Your attorney will prepare documents that accomplish the following:

1. Name a guardian or guardians for your minor children;
2. Name a trusted person to manage the children's money;
3. Implement a Trust or Will that protects your children's inheritance;
4. Name a trusted person to make medical decisions for you if you are unable to make decisions for yourself;
5. Name a trusted person to manage your finances if you become disabled.

What's the Difference Between a Guardian and a Trustee?

A guardian is responsible for the child. A trustee is responsible for the child's money.

How You Name a Guardian

You name a guardian or guardians for your children in a Will.

Who to Choose as Guardian

The following information will help you select a guardian for your minor children. It's sensible to talk to the person(s) you have in mind to make certain they are willing to act as your children's guardian <u>before</u> your attorney prepares the documents.

Most parents strive to name a guardian who shares their values. Elements to consider include the proposed guardian's religious background, lifestyle and living situation.

Since the financial responsibility will rest with a trustee, the guardian's financial qualifications are of lesser importance. Nevertheless your child will certainly be influenced by the guardian's behavior so choosing a person who is financially responsible is important. However if the person named as guardian is also qualified to manage the child's or children's money, the guardian can also be the trustee.

Although nothing prohibits you from appointing someone who resides in another state, take residency into consideration especially if the proposed guardian lives far away from other family members.

Individual vs. a Couple

Parents often name a married couple to be guardians. Consider, however, who would remain the guardian in the event the couple divorces or one member of the couple dies. Often when pressed on this issue, "my sister and brother-in-law" is really "my sister." In the event of your sister's death, do you want your brother-in-law or someone else to be the guardian? Your Will should reflect your true preference by naming only the desired individual or individuals. Nevertheless if a couple is appropriate name them.

A Sibling

You can name an adult child to act as the guardian for your younger children. Although this may help maintain family continuity, it's a substantial responsibility for the older child. In addition to the enormous change moving from the role of older sibling to the role of stand-in parent, the responsibility associated with acting as guardian may put too much pressure on the siblings' relationship. In seeking the best solution for the younger children, this plan has the potential to cause unintended harm to your older child.

How to Protect Your Children's Inheritance

1. Living Trust

As previously discussed, a Living Trust names who is to receive your assets after the death of you and your spouse and who is to administer the trust (the trustee).

As the trustee and beneficiary, you manage and have full use of the trust assets during your lifetime. If you become incompetent and at your death, the person you've named as your successor trustee takes over.

Your attorney will transfer your assets to your trust by changing the title of the asset from your name (and your spouse's name if he or she is also on the title) into the name of your trust.

At your death, your successor trustee will use the trust assets for your children following the guidelines that you have specified in the trust. For example, you may direct your trustee to use the trust assets for your children's support, health, education and welfare. Your guidelines may be quite general or very specific.

The trust will also tell the trustee when to distribute the trust assets that have not been used for the child's health, education etc. You can direct the trustee to make a lump sum payment at the age you specify.

Or you can direct the trustee to make two or more installment payments. Most parents choose to keep the children's inheritance in trust until their children are 21-30 years or older.

Children with Special Needs

If you have a child with "special needs" who receives or may receive government benefits, an inheritance may make the child ineligible for the benefits. A Living Trust with *specific special needs provisions* will safeguard the child's benefits.

Selecting a Trustee

The trustee will be the person responsible for managing and distributing your child's inheritance. Therefore, he or she should have successful financial and investment experience <u>and</u> share your views about money.

The guardian and trustee may be the same person but they don't have to be. The decision is yours. If the guardian and trustee are not the same person, keep in mind that they will have to peacefully co-exist for the benefit of your children for what could be a long time.

Age is also a factor. While the children's grandparents may be the best choice today, as they get older, they may no longer be the best choice.

If your trust will continue after your children turn 18, the guardian will be out of the picture but the Trustee will continue until your youngest child reaches the age you specified in the Trust.

Always, Always Name Backup Guardians and Trustees

For all the reasons I've discussed above, I emphasize naming backups for both the guardian and trustee. Better still, review and revise (if necessary) your estate plan regularly. If you've named grandparents as guardian and/or trustee and that's no longer in your children's best interests, revise your estate plan documents.

Revisions are usually not expensive because you are amending your current documents rather than starting from scratch.

Other Reasons for Using a Living Trust

Trusts are used for reasons other than protecting the finances of minor children. For example: as a married couple trusts can reduce or eliminate estate or death taxes (See Chapter 4.) Trusts are also used to safeguard governmental benefits that are or may be received by disabled children. And trusts, if properly funded, avoid probate.

2. A Will that Creates a Trust at Your Death, Testamentary Trust

A Will that creates a trust at your death (a Testamentary Trust) is an economical alternative to a Living Trust. A Testamentary Trust will accomplish most of the same objectives as a Living Trust. (A Living Trust goes into effect while you're alive. A Testamentary Trust goes into effect at your death.)

Summary of Your Estate Plan

Your estate plan must include a Will because that's how you name guardians for your children. You must then decide to have either a Living Trust or include a Testamentary Trust in the Will. Either option will protect your children's finances. You may, however, have other important objectives that can only be satisfied by a Living Trust. Discuss these options in detail with your attorney.

Final Steps in the Estate Planning Process

Once you have an estate plan in place there are four more steps to take:

1. Place your original will, trust, etc. in a safe place.

2. Inform the person(s) you've named as guardian and trustee, power of attorney, executor or personal representative where they will find

the documents at your death.

3. Make sure that person can access the documents. For example, if you keep these documents in a safe deposit box, will they be able to gain access to the box? If the name of the person who will be managing your affairs is not on the box at your death, they won't have access to your documents.

4. Attach an up-to-date Inventory of your assets and debts to your Will or Trust.

Action Steps

- Ask family, friends or co-workers for the name of an estate planning attorney.
- Schedule an appointment with the attorney and confirm that the initial consultation is free.
- Before you meet with the attorney ask your intended guardian and trustee if they are willing.
- Go to www.wsbforms.com/married and download the forms in the "Take to the Meeting with an Estate Planning Attorney" section. Fill in the blanks and take them to your first meeting with an estate planning attorney.
- Meet with the attorney and discuss your objectives and your options to meet those objectives. Take your Inventory of assets and debts to the meeting.
- If you like the attorney, feel satisfied that you understand your options and the fee is fair, engage the attorney to prepare the documents needed to meet your objectives and create your estate plan.
- Put the documents in a safe place. Tell your family where to find the documents and make certain they can access them.

A Parental Consent Form for Minor Children and a Medical Information Form for Minor Children are available at www.wsbforms.com/married.

SEVEN

ESTATE PLANNING FOR A MARRIED COUPLE WITH ADULT CHILDREN

You will discuss your family structure in detail with your attorney. My goal is to help prepare you for that discussion.

What is an Estate Plan for a Married Couple with Adult Children?

Your attorney will prepare documents that accomplish the following:

1. Name a trusted person to make medical decisions for you if you are unable to make decisions for yourself;
2. Name a trusted person to manage your finances if you become disabled;
3. Transfer your assets to your children at the death of you and your spouse. You have five options:

- Beneficiary Designation;

- Joint Ownership;

-Will;

-No Will;

-Living Trust.

Depending on your circumstances, needs and desires, there are advantages and disadvantages to each of these options. For example, if you have one or two children and the appropriate types of assets, using beneficiary designations and joint ownership may be an economical and effective method of transferring your assets to your children at your death.

On the other hand, if a child has predeceased you, you may (or may not) want your deceased child's share to go to his or her children (your grandchildren). In that case a living trust is the most effective method of transferring your assets.

If you have an adult child with special needs, a revocable living trust with very specific provisions will safeguard any governmental benefits your child receives or may receive in the future.

It may be extremely important to you that your avoid probate for your children. If so, you do not want to transfer your assets to your children by Will.

As you can see, estate planning is **NOT** "one size fits all." That's why I urge you to engage an *experienced* estate planning attorney to prepare your documents.

Final Steps in the Estate Planning Process

Once you have an estate plan in place there are four more steps to take:

1. Place your original will, trust, powers of attorney, etc. in a safe place.

2. Inform the person(s) you've named as trustee, power of attorney, executor or personal representative where they will find the documents at your death or disability.

3. Make sure that person can access the documents. For example, if you keep these documents in a safe deposit box, will they be able to gain access to the box? If the name of the person who will be managing your affairs is not on the box at your death, they won't have access to your documents.

4. Attach an up-to-date Inventory of your assets and debts to your Will or Trust.

Action Steps

- Ask family, friends or co-workers for the name of an estate planning or elder law attorney.

- Schedule an appointment with the attorney and confirm that the initial consultation is free.

- Before you meet with the attorney go to www.wsbforms.com/married and download the forms in the "Take to the Meeting with an Estate Planning Attorney" section. Fill in the blanks and take them to your first meeting with the estate planning attorney.

- Meet with the attorney and discuss your objectives and your options.

- If you like the attorney, feel satisfied that you understand your options and the fee is fair, engage the attorney to prepare the documents needed to create your estate plan.

- Put the documents in a safe place. Tell your children where to find the documents and make certain they can access them.

EIGHT

ESTATE PLANNING FOR A MARRIED COUPLE WITH A "BLENDED" FAMILY

You will discuss your family structure in detail with your attorney. My goal is to help prepare you for that discussion.

Estate Planning for a Blended Family Can be Contentious

Estate Planning for a married couple with a blended family can be a source of conflict for the married couple, their children and even the attorney. You and your spouse may not see eye to eye about who gets what at the first death and again at the second death. This area of estate planning is so complex that you must employ an experienced estate planning attorney. And you may end up employing two attorneys because of the potential for a conflict of interest between spouses.

If you have minor children you will also need to name guardians. Please review the Chapter "Estate Planning for a Married Couple with Minor Children."

Options for Blended Families

- Separate the assets between the spouses and each spouse takes care of his or her own children;
- Take care of your spouse, but make sure your own children eventually get your assets;
- Take care of your spouse and your children, but make sure your children eventually get your assets;
- Both spouses provide for their respective children, each other and their children from the current marriage;
- Leave everything outright to your spouse and then the children of both spouses.

Issues to Consider

- Do both spouses want to transfer their wealth to the children from their first marriage?
- Are there family heirlooms and/or a family business to protect?
- Are both spouses financially independent?
- Will "death taxes" complicate the distribution at the death of the first spouse?
- Will a plan that reduces death taxes also reduce the surviving spouse's control of the money?
- What about the marital residence and the furniture and furnishings; who gets it?
- Will the surviving spouse be able to maintain his or her current standard of living at the death of the first spouse?
- Will the children of the first spouse to die receive "their share" at the death of their parent? Or will they have to wait until the death of their step-parent?
- If the surviving spouse lives for a long time after the death of the first spouse, will the distributions to the children be delayed until the surviving spouse dies? If so, the surviving spouse may not like the idea that stepchildren are eagerly awaiting his or her death to receive their inheritance.

What is an Estate Plan for a Married Couple with a Blended Family?

Your attorney will prepare the documents that accomplish the following:

1. Name a guardian or guardians for your minor children;
2. Name a trusted person to make medical decisions for you if you are unable to make decisions for yourself;
3. Name a trusted person to manage your finances if you become disabled;

4. Transfer your assets to the children at the death of you and your spouse. You have other options but you will probably use beneficiary designation and a living trust or trusts.

Final Steps in the Estate Planning Process

Once you have an estate plan in place there are four more steps to take:

1. Place your original will, trust, powers of attorney, etc. in a safe place.

2. Inform the person(s) you've named as guardian, trustee, power of attorney, executor or personal representative where they will find the documents at your death or disability.

3. Make sure that person can access the documents. For example, if you keep these documents in a safe deposit box, will they be able to gain access to the box? If the name of the person who will be managing your affairs is not on the box at your death, they won't have access to your documents.

4. Attach an up-to-date Inventory of your assets and debts to your Will or Trust.

Action Steps

- Ask family, friends or co-workers for the name of an estate planning or elder law attorney.
- Schedule an appointment with the attorney and confirm that the initial consultation is free.
- Before you meet with the attorney go to www.wsbforms.com/married and download the forms in the "Take to the Meeting with an Estate Planning Attorney" section. Fill in the blanks and take them to your first meeting with an estate planning attorney.

- Meet with the attorney and discuss your objectives and your options.
- If you like the attorney, feel satisfied that you understand your options and the fee is fair, engage the attorney to prepare the documents needed to create your estate plan.
- Put the documents in a safe place. Tell your children where to find the documents and make certain they can access them.

NINE

ESTATE PLANNING FOR A MARRIED COUPLE WITHOUT CHILDREN

You will discuss your family structure in detail with your attorney. My goal is to help prepare you for that discussion.

Estate Planning for a Married Couple Without Children is Critical

Why is it critical? If you and your spouse die without an estate plan in place, your assets will go to the closest living relatives of the second spouse to die. Even if both spouses are in an accident and die within minutes of each other, the family of the spouse who dies last will receive everything.

Who are the closest living relatives? Usually (each state has its own laws that answer this question) it's a parent or parents if they survive you. If not, grandparents if they survive you. If not, it's siblings if they survive you. If none of your siblings survive you it will be the children of deceased siblings, your nieces and nephews.

That means everything you and your spouse worked for and saved could go to someone you haven't seen in years and maybe don't even know. It's foolish to put this off.

If you and your spouse can't decide who should receive your assets, you can leave half to your closest living relatives (legally defined as "heirs at law") and half to your spouse's closest living relatives. Or ou can each name someone to receive your respective half. Or you can name a charity or charities.

What is an Estate Plan for a Married Couple Without Children?

Your attorney will prepare the documents that accomplish the following:

1. Name a trusted person to make medical decisions for you if you are unable to make decisions for yourself;
2. Name a trusted person to manage your finances if you become disabled;
3. Transfer your assets to the individuals of your choice at the death of you and your spouse. You have four options:

- Beneficiary Designation;

- Joint Ownership;

-Will;

-Living Trust.

Final Steps in the Estate Planning Process

Once you have an estate plan in place there are four more steps to take:

1. Place your original will, trust, powers of attorney, etc. in a safe place.

2. Inform the person(s) you've named as trustee, power of attorney, executor or personal representative where they will find the documents at your death or disability.

3. Make sure that person can access the documents. For example, if you keep these documents in a safe deposit box, will they be able to gain access to the box? If the name of the person who will be managing your affairs is not on the box at your death, they won't have access to your documents.

4. Attach an up-to-date Inventory of your assets and debts to your Will or Trust.

Action Steps

- Ask family, friends or co-workers for the name of an estate planning or elder law attorney.
- Schedule an appointment with the attorney and confirm that the initial consultation is free.
- Before you meet with the attorney go to www.wsbforms.com/married and download the forms in the "Take to the Meeting with an Estate Planning Attorney" section. Fill in the blanks and take them to your first meeting with an estate planning attorney.
- Meet with the attorney and discuss your objectives and your options.
- If you like the attorney, feel satisfied that you understand your options and the fee is fair, engage the attorney to prepare the documents needed to create your estate plan.
- Put the documents in a safe place. Tell your family member or friend that you've named in your documents where to find the documents and make certain they can access them.

TEN

CONGRATULATIONS!
NOW THAT YOU HAVE YOUR AFFAIRS IN
ORDER, KEEP THEM IN ORDER

You should discuss this issue in detail with your attorney. My goal is to prepare you for that discussion.

Keep Your Affairs Up-To-Date

Now that your financial and legal affairs are in order, keep them up-to-date.

Schedule periodic reviews of:

Assets and debts,

Insurance policies,

Pension\retirement plans,

Estate plan,

Tax matters.

Review these issues yearly and at all family events that change your circumstances, i.e. marriage or remarriage, births, death, divorce, employment changes, retirement and the purchase or sale of significant assets.

Schedule Reviews

Incorporate periodic reviews of your financial and legal affairs into your day planner or diary system. But reminding yourself to review a specific financial or legal matter is useless if you don't actually review it and make any necessary changes.

The Location of Your Documents and Other Important Information

Your objectives are to:

1. Provide information to your family about your doctors, other health personnel and your medications.

2. Provide information to your family about the people to contact in an emergency.

3. Provide information to your family about your financial and legal advisors.

4. Provide information to your family about a prearranged funeral and\or burial.

Go to www.wsbforms.com/married/ and download the Location of Important Documents form. Fill in the information and then place the list in a secure but accessible place. Tell your spouse or children where to find the information and make certain they can gain access. For example, if you place the list in your safe deposit box, be sure your spouse, children or family member know where the box is, where to find the key and are named on the bank's signature card.

Records Stored in Your Computer

If some of your records are stored in your computer:

Make a backup of these records and put the backup in a safe place; *a place that you will remember.*

Prepare a set of instructions for your spouse or family so they will be able to access this information. A detailed computer file of important information is useless if your family doesn't know it exists or knows it exists but can't find it or gain access to it.

Pay special attention to your passwords if you bank on-line.

Action Plan

- Schedule and actually review: Assets and Debts, Estate Tax liability, Insurance, Retirement and Estate Plan.
- Make changes as necessary.
- Attach an up-to-date Inventory of your assets and debts, life insurance policies and retirement plans to your estate plan documents.
- Inform your spouse and children of the location of the safe place and make certain they can access the documents.
- Inform spouse and children about documents stored on your computer and how to access the documents.

Get started.

"Knowledge is Power" but only if the knowledge prompts action. That's why this estate planning guide provides not only accurate up-to-date information but also the action steps required to achieve your objectives.

As in most important undertakings the first step is ALWAYS the most difficult. But once you get started everything will quickly fall into place. Your reward will be the peace of mind that comes from knowing that you have made things as easy as possible for your children and that your affairs are in order.

ABOUT THE AUTHOR

Julie Calligaro has been an estate planning and probate attorney for 30 years. An estate planning attorney is really in the peace of mind business because once a married couple has their affairs in order, they will experience peace of mind.

Ms. Calligaro was named an Estate and Gift Taxation Lawyer of the year by *"dbusiness,"* Detroit's premier business journal, in 2010. And has been a member of the Ethics Committee at Henry Ford Wyandotte Hospital for 17 years.